TO:
Dr. Copeland

Thank you for
all of your support
and help! Your
experiences and
genuine care and
concern for others
brings great joy
to my soul and
spirit.
Thank you :)

From: Marie
Humphrey

EXPRESSIONS
OF *Joy*

EXPRESSIONS

OF *Joy*

Helen Steiner Rice

BARBOUR
PUBLISHING

© 2007 by the Helen Steiner Rice Foundation

ISBN 978-1-59789-828-7

Devotional writing by Rebecca Currington in association with Snapdragon Group ℠ Editorial Services.

The poetry of Helen Steiner Rice is published under a licensing agreement with the Helen Steiner Rice Foundation.

Special thanks to Virginia Ruehlmann for her cooperation and assistance in the development of this book.

All rights reserved. No part of this publication may be reproduced or transmitted for commercial purposes, except for brief quotations in printed reviews, without written permission of the publisher.

Churches and other noncommercial interests may reproduce portions of this book without the express written permission of Barbour Publishing, provided that the text does not exceed 500 words or 5 percent of the entire book, whichever is less, and that the text is not material quoted from another publisher. When reproducing text from this book, include the following credit line: "From *Expressions of Joy*, published by Barbour Publishing, Inc. Used by permission."

All scripture quotations, unless otherwise indicated, are taken from the HOLY BIBLE, NEW INTERNATIONAL VERSION®. NIV®. Copyright © 1973, 1978, 1984 by International Bible Society. Used by permission of Zondervan. All rights reserved.

Scripture quotations marked NLT are taken from the *Holy Bible*, New Living Translation, copyright © 1996, 2006. Used by permission of Tyndale House Publishers, Inc., Wheaton, Illinois 60189, U.S.A. All rights reserved.

Published by Barbour Publishing, Inc., P.O. Box 719, Uhrichsville, Ohio 44683
www.barbourbooks.com

Our mission is to publish and distribute inspirational products offering exceptional value and biblical encouragement to the masses.

Printed in Malaysia.

Contents

In Nature

You will live in joy and peace. The mountains and hills will burst into song, and the trees of the field will clap their hands!

ISAIAH 55:12 NLT

God's gifts are all around you, dear friend. Picture your heavenly Father fashioning each flower, each tree, each star, each bird on the wing. Can you see Him smiling as He creates these beautiful gifts for His children? Look around you—*really look*. See what He has done. Then lift up your hands and your voice. Let Him see and hear that you appreciate His handiwork. Let Him see what joy His gifts have brought to your life.

7

Each time you look up in the sky

Or watch the fluffy clouds drift by,

Or feel the sunshine warm and bright,

Or watch the dark night turn to light,

Or hear a bluebird sweetly sing,

Or see the winter turn to spring,

Or touch a leaf or see a tree,

It's all God whispering, "This is Me..."

Through all of creation

    with symphonic splendor

God speaks with a voice

    that is gentle and tender.

And the birds in the trees

    and the flowers of spring

All join in proclaiming

    this heavenly King.

*Though you have not seen him,
you love him; and even though you
do not see him now, you believe
in him and are filled with an
inexpressible and glorious joy.*

I PETER 1:8

*H*e's the stars in the heaven,

a smile on some face,

A leaf on a tree or a rose in a vase.

He's winter and autumn

and summer and spring,

In short, God is every real

and wonderful thing.

You ask me how I know it's true

that there is a living God.

A God who rules the universe—

the sky, the sea, the sod—

A God who hangs the sun out slowly

with the break of day

And gently takes the stars

in and puts the night away.

What better answers are there

to prove His holy being

Than the wonders all around us

that are ours just for the seeing.

Apple blossoms bursting wide

  now beautify the tree

And make a springtime picture

  that is beautiful to see.

As the flowering branches

  depend upon the tree

To nourish and fulfill them

  till they reach futurity,

We, too, must be dependent

  on our Father up above,

For we are but the branches

  and He's the tree of love.

After the winter comes the spring
To show us again that in everything

There's always a renewal divinely planned,

Flawlessly perfect, the work of God's hand.

God lives in the beauty

    that comes with spring—

The colorful flowers,

    the birds that sing—

And He lives in people as kind as you,

And He lives in all the nice things you do.

APRIL COMES WITH CHEEKS A-GLOWING

SILVER STREAMS ARE ALL A-FLOWING,

FLOWERS OPEN WIDE THEIR EYES

IN LOVELY RAPTUROUS SURPRISE.

LILIES DREAM BESIDE THE BROOKS,

VIOLETS IN MEADOW NOOKS,

AND THE BIRDS GONE WILD WITH GLEE

FILL THE WOODS WITH MELODY.

Flowers sleeping 'neath the snow,
Awakening when the spring winds blow,
Leafless trees so bare before
Gowned in lacy green once more,
Hard, unyielding, frozen sod
Now softly carpeted by God;
Still streams melting in the spring,
Rippling over rocks that sing,
Barren, windswept, lonely hills
Turning gold with daffodils—
These miracles are all around,
Within our sight and touch and sound,
As true and wonderful today
As when the stone was rolled away,
Proclaiming to all doubting men
That in God all things live again.

Springtime is a season of

　　hope and joy and cheer—

There's beauty all around us

　　to see and touch and hear. . .

So no matter how downhearted and

　　discouraged we may be,

New hope is born when we behold

　　leaves budding on a tree

Or when we see a timid flower

　　push through the frozen sod

And open wide in glad surprise

　　its petaled eyes to God.

I come to meet You, God, and as I linger here

I seem to feel You very near.

A rustling leaf, a rolling slope

Speak to my heart of endless hope.

The sun just rising in the sky,

The waking birdlings as they fly,

The grass all wet with morning dew

Are telling me I just met You. . .

Gently, thus the day is born

As night gives way to breaking morn,

And once again I've met You, God,

And worshipped on Your holy sod. . .

For who could see the dawn break through

Without a glimpse of heaven and You?

For who but God could make the day

And softly put the night away?

I see the dew glisten

in crystal-like splendor

While God, with a touch

that is gentle and tender,

Wraps up the night

and softly tucks it away

And hangs out the sun

to herald a new day.

*D*ear God, there are things

we cannot measure

Like the depths and waves of sea

And the heights of stars in heaven

And the joy You bring to me.

In Faith

Though you have not seen him, you love him;
and even though you do not see him now,
you believe in him and are filled with an
inexpressible and glorious joy.

1 PETER 1:8

Joy—the kind God gives—is a faith thing.
As you receive by faith what God has
provided for you, your joy grows. As you
slip your hand in His and walk in faith,
believing that His paths are good, your joy
thrives regardless of the circumstances
in your life. As you place your burdens,
your future, your limitations, your pride,
your hopes and fears in His hands, the joy
of the Lord will fill every corner of your
heart.

$\mathcal{F}$aith to believe when

the way is rough

And faith to hang on

when the going is tough

Will never fail to pull us through

And bring us strength and comfort, too.

FAITH MAKES IT WHOLLY POSSIBLE

TO QUIETLY ENDURE

THE VIOLENT WORLD AROUND US,

FOR IN GOD WE ARE SECURE.

All we really ever need

Is faith as a grain of mustard seed,

For all God asks is that you believe.

For if you do, ye shall receive.

Take heart and meet each minute

with faith in God's great love,

Aware that every day of life

is controlled by God above. . .

And never dread tomorrow

or what the future brings—

Just pray for strength and courage

and trust God in all things.

"For I know the plans I have for you," declares the LORD, *"plans to prosper you and not to harm you, plans to give you hope and a future."*

JEREMIAH 29:11

When the darkness shuts out the light,

We must lean on faith to restore our sight,

For there is nothing we need to know

If we have faith that wherever we go

God will be there to help us bear

Our disappointments, pain, and care.

No day is too dark and

   no burden too great

That God in His love cannot penetrate. . .

And to know and believe

   without question or doubt

That no matter what happens

   God is there to help out

Is to hold in your hand the golden key

To peace and joy and serenity.

Oh, Father, grant once more to men

A simple, childlike faith again,

Forgetting color, race, and creed

And seeing only the heart's deep need. . .

For faith alone can save man's soul

And lead him to a higher goal,

For there's but one unfailing course—

We win by faith and not by force.

For with patience to wait

    and faith to endure,

Your life will be blessed

    and your future secure,

For God is but testing

    your faith and your love

Before He appoints you to rise far above

All the small things that

    so sorely distress you,

For God's only intention is

    to strengthen and bless you.

It's easy to grow downhearted

  when nothing goes your way.

It's easy to be discouraged

  when you have a troublesome day.

But trouble is only a challenge

  to spur you on to achieve

The best that God has to offer

  if you have the faith to believe.

FAITH IS A FORCE THAT IS GREATER

THAN KNOWLEDGE OR POWER OR SKILL,

AND THE DARKEST DEFEAT TURNS TO TRIUMPH

IF YOU TRUST IN GOD'S WISDOM AND WILL,

FOR FAITH IS A MOVER OF MOUNTAINS—

THERE'S NOTHING MAN CANNOT ACHIEVE

IF HE HAS THE COURAGE TO TRY IT

AND THEN HAS THE FAITH TO BELIEVE.

Though I cannot find Your hand

To lead me on to the promised land,

I still believe with all my being

Your hand is there beyond my seeing.

*"Blessed are those who have not seen
and yet have believed."*

JOHN 20:29

Nothing is ever too hard to do

If your faith is strong

and your purpose is true. . .

So never give up, and never stop—

Just journey on to the mountaintop!

In a small child's shining eyes

The faith of all ages lies. . .

And tiny hands and tousled heads

That kneel in prayer by little beds.

In Prayer

This is the confidence we have in approaching God: that if we ask anything according to his will, he hears us. And if we know that he hears us—whatever we ask—we know that we have what we asked of him.

1 JOHN 5:14–15

Prayer is first and foremost a conversation between two parties—you and Almighty God. Imagine what privilege that affords, for there is no higher court, no ear more ready to listen than His. Bring Him your requests, place them at His feet, and then linger long in His presence. Oh what joy you will experience knowing that He has the power to do the impossible. Go to Him often in prayer. He welcomes you.

43

It fills me with joy

just to linger with You,

As my soul You replenish

and my heart You renew.

So thank You again

for your mercy and love

And for making me heir

to Your kingdom above.

So kneel in prayer in His presence,
    and you'll find no need to speak;
For softly in quiet communion,
    God grants you the peace that you seek.

Prayer is so often just words unspoken,

Whispered in tears by a heart that is broken,

For God is already deeply aware

Of the burdens we find too heavy to bear. . .

And all we need do is seek Him in prayer,

And without a word He will help us to bear

Our trials and troubles,

   our sickness and sorrow,

And show us the way to a brighter tomorrow.

There's no need at all for impressive prayer,

For the minute we seek God

   He's already there.

Whenever we're troubled

and lost in despair,

We have but to seek Him

and ask Him in prayer

To guide and direct us

and help us to bear

Our sickness and sorrow,

our worry and care.

Teach me to do your will,
for you are my God; may your good
Spirit lead me on level ground.

PSALM 143:10

Though we feel helpless

and alone when we start,

A prayer is the key that opens the heart,

And as the heart opens,

the dear Lord comes in

And the prayer that we felt

we could never begin

Is so easy to say,

for the Lord understands

And He gives us new strength

by the touch of His hands.

*O*n the wings of prayer

  our burdens take flight

And our load of care

  becomes bearably light

And our heavy hearts are lifted above

To be healed by the balm

  of God's wonderful love. . .

I cannot dwell apart from You—

You would not ask or want me to,

For You have room within Your heart

To make each child of Yours a part

Of You and all Your love and care

If we but come to You in prayer.

My garden beautifies my yard

and adds fragrance to the air. . .

But it is also my cathedral

and my quiet place of prayer. . .

So little do we realize that

the glory and the power

Of Him who made the universe

lies hidden in a flower.

Just close your eyes and open your heart

And feel your worries and cares depart,

Just yield yourself to the Father above

And let Him hold you secure in His love.

So when you are tired, discouraged, and blue,

There's always one door that is open to you—

For the heart is a temple when God is there

As we place ourselves in His loving care.

Brighten your day

And lighten your way

And lessen your cares

With daily prayers.

Quiet your mind

And leave tension behind

And find inspiration

In hushed meditation.

For when we seek shelter

in His wondrous love,

And we ask Him to send us

help from above. . .

And that is the reason we know it is true

That bright, shining hours

and dark, sad ones, too,

Are part of the plan God made for each one,

And all we can pray is, "Thy will be done."

And know that you are never alone,

For God is your Father

and you're one of His own.

To you, O Lord, I lift up my soul.

PSALM 25:1

Although it sometimes seems to us

   our prayers have not been heard,

God always knows our every need

   without a single word,

And He will not forsake us,

   a tender watch to keep. . .

And in good time He'll answer us,

   and in His love He'll send

Greater things than we have asked

   and blessings without end.

Whenever I am troubled

and lost in deep despair,

I bundle all my troubles up

and go to God in prayer. . .

I know He stilled the tempest

and calmed the angry sea,

And I humbly ask if, in His love,

He'll do the same for me. . .

And then I just keep quiet

and think only thoughts of peace,

And as I abide in stillness

my restless murmurings cease.

There is only one place

and only one friend

Who is never too busy,

and you can always depend

On Him to be waiting,

with arms open wide,

To hear all the troubles

you came to confide.

For the heavenly Father

will always be there

When you seek Him and find Him

at the altar of prayer.

I said a special prayer for you—

I asked the Lord above

To keep you safely in His care

and enfold you in His love.

I did not ask for fortune,

for riches or for fame,

I only asked for blessings

in the Holy Savior's name—

Blessings to surround you

in time of trial and stress,

And inner joy to fill your heart

with peace and happiness.

Prayers are the stairs that lead to God,

and there's joy every step of the way

When we make our pilgrimage to Him

with love in our hearts each day.

"Ask and it will be given to you;
seek and you will find; knock and
the door will be opened to you."

MATTHEW 7:7

There's no problem too big

and no question too small—

Just ask God in faith,

and He'll answer them all—

Not always at once,

so be patient and wait,

For God never comes

too soon or too late. . .

So trust in His wisdom

and believe in His Word,

For no prayer's unanswered

and no prayer's unheard.

All of our errors and failures

that we made in the course of the day

Are freely forgiven at nighttime

when we kneel down and earnestly pray,

So seek the Lord in the morning

and never forget Him at night,

For prayer is an unfailing blessing

that makes every burden seem light.

In Times of Trial

Let us hold tightly without wavering to the hope we affirm, for God can be trusted to keep his promise.

HEBREWS 10:23 NLT

Is it possible to be joyful even in the face of trials and tribulations? It is, dear friend! When your faith is tried, it grows stronger, more mature and resilient because it allows God to demonstrate His love and His faithfulness to you. These triumphs may not come in the packages you expect, but they are fashioned by God's wisdom and understanding. Rejoice, dear friend, even in your trials.

When you're troubled and

worried and sick at heart

And your plans are upset

and your world falls apart,

Remember God's ready

and waiting to share

The burden you find too heavy to bear.

Life can't always be a song—

You have to have trouble

　to make you strong,

So whenever you are troubled

　and everything goes wrong,

It is just God working in you

　to make your spirit strong.

Nothing in life can defeat me,

For as long as this knowledge remains,

I can suffer whatever is happening,

For I know God will break all the chains

That are binding me tight in the darkness

And trying to fill me with fear. . .

For there is no night without dawning,

And I know that my morning is near.

God never plows in the soul of man
Without intention and
    purpose and plan. . .
So whenever you feel
    the plow's sharp blade
Let not your heart be sorely afraid,
For, like the farmer, God chooses a field
From which He expects
    an excellent yield. . .
So rejoice though your heart
    be broken in two—
God seeks to bring forth
    a rich harvest in you.

> "*I have told you these things,*
> *so that in me you may have peace.*
> *In this world you will have trouble.*
> *But take heart! I have overcome the world.*"

No one discovers the fullness
    or the greatness of God's love
Unless they have walked in the darkness
    with only a light from above. . .
For the failure to endure whatever comes
    is born of sorrow and trials
And strengthened only by discipline
    and nurtured by self-denials;
So be not disheartened by troubles,
    for trials are the building blocks
On which to erect a fortress of faith,
    secure on God's ageless rocks.

He is our shepherd, our Father, our guide,

And you're never alone

with the Lord at your side. . .

So may the Great Physician attend you,

And may His healing completely mend you.

With faith in your heart,

    reach out for God's hand

And accept what He sends,

    though you can't understand. . .

For our Father in heaven

    always knows what is best,

And if you trust in His wisdom,

    your life will be blessed. . .

For always remember that

    whatever betide you,

You are never alone,

    for God is beside you.

When life seems empty

and there's no place to go,

When your heart is troubled

and your spirits are low

When friends seem few and nobody cares

There is always God to hear your prayers.

So go to our Father when troubles assail you,

For His grace is sufficient

and He'll never fail you.

Growing trees are strengthened
  when they withstand the storm,
And the sharp cut of a chisel
  gives the marble grace and form.
God never hurts us needlessly
  and He never wastes our pain,
For every loss He sends to us
  is followed by rich gain.
So whenever we are troubled
  and when everything goes wrong,
It is just God working in us
  to make our spirits strong.

We love the sound of laughter

and the merriment of cheer,

But our hearts would lose their tenderness

if we never shed a tear. . .

So whenever we are troubled

and life has lost its song

It's God testing us with burdens

just to make our spirit strong!

Never dread tomorrow

　　or what the future brings

Just pray for strength and courage

　　and trust God in all things,

And never grow discouraged—

　　be patient and just wait,

For God never comes too early,

　　and He never comes too late.

The LORD is my strength and my
shield; my heart trusts in him, and I
am helped. My heart leaps for joy and
I will give thanks to him in song.

PSALM 28:7

In My Salvation

*Anyone who belongs to Christ has become
a new person. The old life is gone;
a new life has begun!*

2 CORINTHIANS 5:17 NLT

Nothing brings more joy to the human
heart than God's salvation, and nothing
brings more joy to God's heart than those
who receive His amazing gift. We were
given the power of choice, and we chose
to walk away—but He did not! He paid
the price for our sin and redeemed us. Joy
is knowing that each of us has been given
a second chance to be God's child.

I ask myself,

Just who am I

That God should send His only Son

That my salvation would be won

Upon a cross by a sinless man

To bring fulfillment to God's Plan—

For Jesus suffered, bled, and died

That sinners might be sanctified,

And to grant God's children, such as I,

Eternal life in that home on high.

Open your heart's door

and let Christ come in,

And He'll give you new life

and free you from sin—

And there is no joy

that can ever compare

With the joy of knowing

you're in God's care.

The Lord is our salvation

And our strength in every fight,

Our redeemer and protector,

Our eternal guiding light. . .

He has promised to sustain us,

He's our refuge from all harms,

And underneath this refuge

Are the everlasting arms.

I am often weak and weary,

and life is dark and bleak and dreary. . .

But somehow when I realize

that He who made the sea and skies

And holds the whole world in His hand

has my small soul in His command,

It gives me strength to try once more

to somehow reach the heavenly door

Where I will live forevermore

with friends and loved ones I adore.

*Finally, brothers, whatever is true,
whatever is noble, whatever is right,
whatever is pure, whatever is lovely,
whatever is admirable—if anything
is excellent or praiseworthy—
think about such things.*

PHILIPPIANS 4:8

THOSE WHO BELIEVE IN WHAT THE SAVIOR SAID

WILL RISE IN GLORY THOUGH THEY BE DEAD. . .

SO DEATH COMES TO US JUST TO OPEN THE DOOR

TO THE KINGDOM OF GOD AND LIFE EVERMORE.

Step by step we climb day by day

Closer to God with each prayer we pray,

For the cry of the heart offered in prayer

Becomes just another spiritual stair

In the heavenly staircase leading us to

A beautiful place where we live anew.

*N*ever give up,

for it's worth the climb

To live forever in endless time

Where the soul of man is safe and free

To live and love through eternity.

I am the Way, so just follow Me

Though the way be rough

and you cannot see. . .

I am the Truth which all men seek,

So heed not false prophets

or the words that they speak. . .

I am the Life, and I hold the key

That opens the door to eternity. . .

And in this dark world, I am the Light

To the Promised Land

where there is no night.

He carried the cross to Calvary—

Carried its burden for you and me.

There on the cross He was crucified,

And because He bled and died,

We know that whatever our cross may be,

It leads to God and eternity.

For all who believe in the risen Lord
Have been assured of this reward,
And death for them is just graduation
To a higher realm of wide elevation—
For life on earth is a transient affair,
Just a few brief years in which to prepare
For a life that is free from pain and tears
Where time is not counted by hours or years.

If you are searching to find the way

To life everlasting and eternal day,

With faith in your heart

   take the path that He trod,

For the way of the cross is the way to God.

> *"For God so loved the world that he gave his one and only Son, that whoever believes in him shall not perish but have eternal life."*

JOHN 3:16

In Peace

The peace of God, which transcends all understanding, will guard your hearts and your minds in Christ Jesus.

PHILIPPIANS 4:7

The whole world longs for peace to no avail, because true peace is God's gift. It comes when we relinquish ourselves to Him, when we lay our burdens at His feet, when we invest our faith in His greatness. The heart at peace is a joyful heart, a heart that knows its creator's love, a heart that knows its future is settled in the arms of God. Open your heart, dear friend, and receive Him—the Prince of Peace.

This brings you a million

   good wishes and more

For the things you cannot buy

   in a store—

Like faith to sustain you

   in times of trial,

A joy-filled heart, and a happy smile,

Contentment, inner peace, and love—

All priceless gifts from God above!

May peace and understanding

Give you strength and courage, too,

And may the hours and the days ahead

Hold a new hope for you;

For the sorrow that is yours today

Will pass away and then

You'll find the sun of happiness

Will shine for you again.

Take the Savior's loving hand

And do not try to understand—

Just let Him lead you where He will,

Through pastures green and waters still.

*"Blessed rather are those who hear
the word of God and obey it."*

LUKE 11:28

I come to You when day is done

And find You waiting there,

And with Your magic fingertips

The heavy robe of care

Slips from the heart;

And roses bloom,

Because Your presence

Fills the room.

While God's almighty power

   is not ours to understand,

We know who holds the future

   and we know who holds our hand—

And to have the steadfast knowledge

   that we never walk alone

And to rest in the assurance

   that our every need is known

Will help dispel our worries,

   and in trusting Him we'll find

Right in the midst of chaos

   God can give us peace of mind.

THOUGH THE WAY AHEAD SEEMS STEEP,

BE NOT AFRAID FOR HE WILL KEEP

TENDER WATCH THROUGH NIGHT AND DAY,

AND HE WILL HEAR EACH PRAYER YOU PRAY.

If we but had the eyes to see

God's face in every cloud,

If we but had the ears to hear

His voice above the crowd,

We'd find the peace we're seeking,

the kind no man can give—

The peace that comes from knowing

He died so we might live!

After the clouds, the sunshine,

After the winter, the spring,

After the shower, the rainbow,

For life is a changeable thing.

After the night, the morning,

Bidding all darkness cease,

After life's cares and sorrows,

The comfort of sweetness and peace.

So kneel in prayer in His presence,

and you'll find no need to speak;

For softly in quiet communion,

God grants you the peace that you seek.

When your nervous network

becomes a tangled mess,

Just close your eyes in silent prayer

and ask the Lord to bless

Each thought that you are thinking,

each decision you must make,

As well as every word you speak

and every step you take—

For only by the grace of God

can you gain self-control,

And only meditative thoughts

can restore your peace of soul.

God bless you most abundantly

with joys that never cease,

The joy of knowing that He came

to bring the whole world peace.

Do not be anxious, said our Lord,

Have peace from day to day—

The lilies neither toil nor spin,

Yet none are clothed as they.

The meadowlark with sweetest song

Fears not for bread or nest,

Because he trusts our Father's love

And God knows what is best.

When life becomes a problem

much too great for us to bear,

Instead of trying to escape,

let us withdraw in prayer—

For withdrawal means renewal

if we withdraw to pray

And listen in the quietness

to hear what God will say.

In My Family

*"A new command I give you:
Love one another. As I have loved you,
so you must love one another."*

JOHN 13:34

Ah. . .family. What greater blessing do
we have here on earth than the sweet
voices and familiar faces of those we
love? They are our companions on the
journey of life, adding to our joy. We are
also part of God's family—one of a vast
number of sisters and brothers in the
Lord; loving, laughing, encouraging, and
supporting one another. Our hearts are
filled with gratefulness and praise to our
God for His goodness.

In seeking peace for all people

There is only one place to begin,

And that is in each home and heart—

For the fortress of peace is within.

Where there is love the heart is light,

Where there is love the day is bright,

Where there is love there is a song

To help when things are going wrong. . .

And where the home is filled with love

You'll always find God spoken of,

And when a family prays together,

That family also stays together.

*M*emories to treasure are

made every day—

Made of family gatherings

and children as they play.

In my eyes there lies no vision

but the sight of your dear face.

In my heart there is no feeling

but the warmth of your embrace.

In my mind there are no thoughts

but the thoughts of you, my dear.

In my soul, no other longing

but just to have you near.

All my dreams were built around you,

and I've come to know it's true:

In my life there is no living

that is not part of you.

Above all, love each other
deeply, because love covers
over a multitude of sins.

1 PETER 4:8

It is sharing and caring,
Giving and forgiving,
Loving and being loved,
Walking hand in hand,
Talking heart to heart,
Seeing through each other's eyes,
Laughing together,
Weeping together,
Praying together,
And always trusting and believing
And thanking God for each other. . .
For love that is shared is a beautiful thing—
It enriches the soul and makes the heart sing.

There's a road I call Remembrance

where I walk each day with you.

It's a pleasant, happy road, my dear,

all filled with memories true.

Today it leads me through a spot

where I can dream awhile,

And in its tranquil peacefulness

I touch your hand and smile.

There are hills and fields and budding trees

and stillness that's so sweet.

That it seems that this must be the place

where God and humans meet.

I hope we can go back again

and golden hours renew,

And God go with you always, dear,

until the day we do.

It takes a mother's kindness

to forgive us when we err,

To sympathize in trouble

and bow her head in prayer.

It takes a mother's wisdom

to recognize our needs

And to give us reassurance

by her loving words and deeds.

Time cannot destroy the memory

and years can never erase

The tenderness and the beauty

of the love in a mother's face.

And when we think of our mothers,

we draw nearer to God above,

For only God in His greatness

could fashion a mother's love.

A baby is a gift of life
    born of the wonder of love—
A little bit of eternity
    sent from the Father above,
Giving a new dimension to the love
    between husband and wife
And putting an added new meaning
    to the wonder and mystery of life.
Each flower a message is bringing,
    a memory of someone dear
A picture of deepest devotion
    dispelling all doubt and fear.
Amid all this beauty and splendor,
    one flower stands forth as queen—
For never a flower existed
    like the blossom I can claim.
For after years I now can see
    amid life's roses and rue
God's greatest gift to a little child,
    my darling mother, was you.

A wee bit of heaven

    drifted down from above—

A handful of happiness,

    a heart full of love.

The mystery of life so sacred and sweet,

The giver of joy so deep and complete.

Precious and priceless, so lovable, too—

The world's sweetest miracle,

    baby, is you.

"Train a child in the way he should go, and when he is old he will not turn from it."

PROVERBS 22:6

Tender little memories

of some word or deed

Give us strength and courage

when we are in need.

Blessed little memories

help to bear the cross

And soften all the bitterness

of failure and of loss.

Precious little memories

of little things we've done

Make the very darkest day

a bright and happy one.

Ten little fingers, ten little toes,

Tiny as a minute, sweet as a rose—

One of life's mysteries,

which nobody knows,

And one of the miracles

only God can disclose.

In God's Love

God is love. Whoever lives in love lives in God, and God in him.

1 JOHN 4:16

The Bible says that love is the greatest of all virtues—and it must be true, for that is where all others begin and end. It was God's love that caused Him to create us and His love that bought us back when sin separated us from Him. It is His love in our hearts that fuels kindness, gentleness, meekness, faith, and joy in our lives. God's love surrounds you, dear friend.

A warm, ready smile
　　　or a kind, thoughtful deed
Or a hand outstretched in
　　　an hour of need
Can change our whole outlook
　　　and make the world bright
Where a minute before
　　　just nothing seemed right—
It's a wonderful world
　　　and it always will be
If we keep our eyes open
　　　and focused to see
The wonderful things man is capable of
When he opens his heart
　　　to God and His love.

Don't doubt for a minute

    that this is not true,

For God loves His children

    and takes care of them, too. . .

And all of His treasures

    are yours to share

If you love Him completely

    and show that you care. . .

And if you walk in His footsteps

    and have faith to believe,

There's nothing you ask for

    that you will not receive.

No matter what your past has been,

Trust God to understand.

And no matter what your problem is

Just place it in His hand—

For in all of our unloveliness,

He loved us since the world began

And what's more, He always will.

God's love is like an island in

life's ocean vast and wide—

A peaceful, quiet shelter from

the restless, rising tide. . .

God's love is like a fortress,

and we seek protection there

When the waves of tribulation

seem to drown us in despair. . .

God's love is like a beacon burning

bright with faith and prayer

And through the changing scenes of life

we can find a haven there!

We are all God's children

and He loves us, every one.

He freely and completely forgives

all that we have done,

Asking only if we're ready

to where He leads,

Content that in His wisdom

He answer all our needs.

What is love? No words can define it—

It's something so great

only God could design it.

For love means much more

than small words can express,

For what we call love is very much less

Than the beauty and depth

and the true richness of

God's gift to mankind—

His compassionate love.

*K*ings and kingdoms all pass away—

Nothing on earth endures. . .

But the love of God who sent His Son

Is forever and ever yours!

Somebody loves you more than you know,

Somebody goes with you wherever you go,

Somebody really and truly cares

And lovingly listens

    to all of your prayers.

And if you walk in His footsteps

    and have faith to believe,

There's nothing you ask for

    that you will not receive.

"If you believe, you will receive whatever you ask for in prayer."

Wait with a heart that is patient

For the goodness of God to prevail—

For never do prayers go unanswered,

And His mercy and love never fail.

*In all these things we are more
than conquerors through him
who loves us.*

ROMANS 8:37

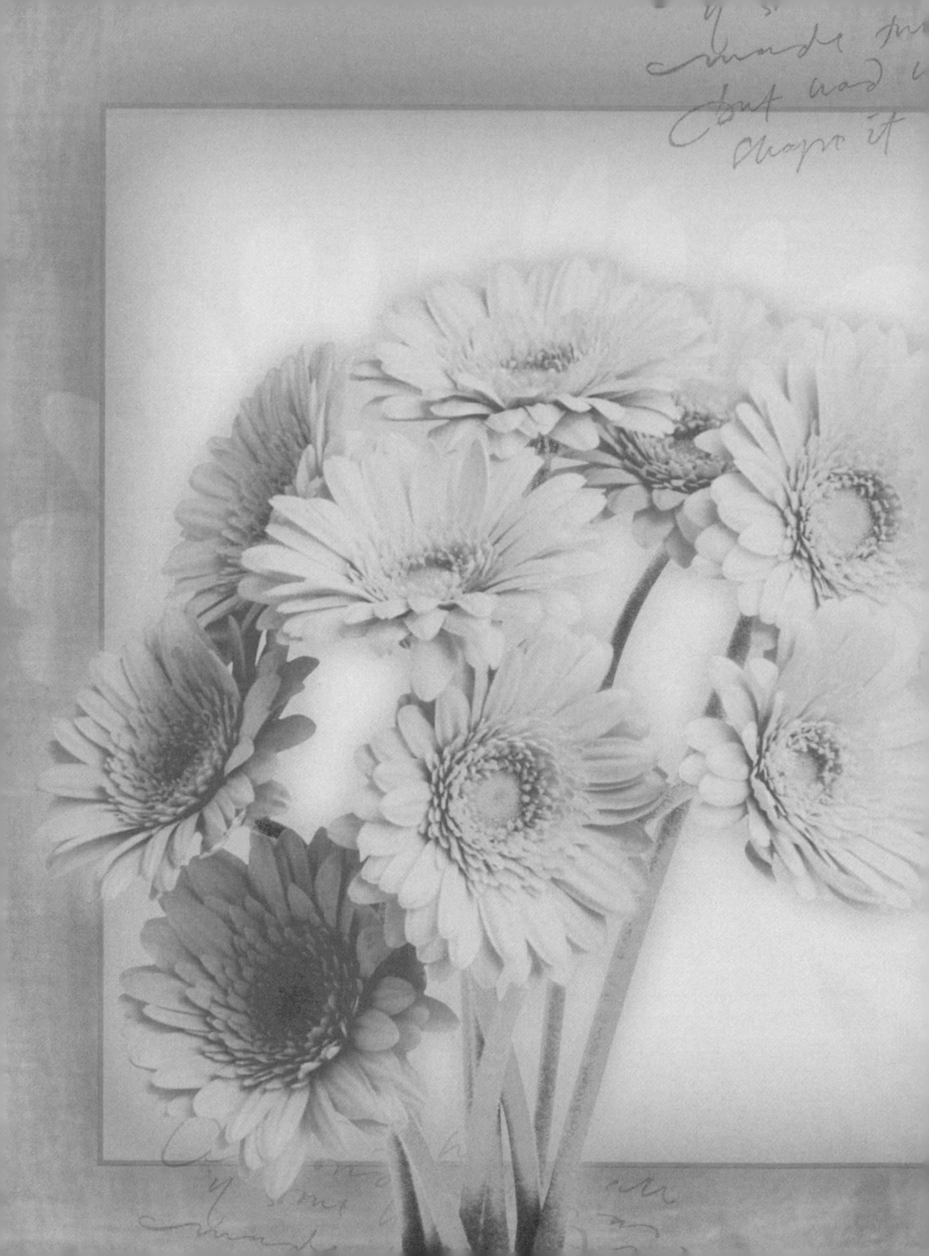

In My Friends

Dear friends, let us continue to love one another, for love comes from God. Anyone who loves is a child of God and knows God.

1 JOHN 4:7 NLT

Friends are a priceless gift. Without the obligation of kin, they choose to be there for you when skies are fair and when stormy winds blow. They hold your hand when you are suffering and share your joy when blessings flow. Embrace your friends and hold them close, for they are more precious than silver or gold. They sparkle more brightly than diamonds. Treasure them. And strive to be the best friend you can be to them.

made for
but used
chaps it

Across the years we've met in dreams

And shared each other's hopes and schemes,

We knew a friendship rich and rare

And beauty far beyond compare.

Then you reached out your arms for more,

To catch what you were yearning for.

But little did you think or guess

That one can't capture happiness

Because it's unrestrained and free,

Unfettered by reality.

Who can say just what

makes a friend

Or why one heart and

another blend?

Life is like a garden

And friendship like a flower

That blooms and grows in beauty

With the sunshine and the shower.

And in the garden of the heart,

Friendship's flower opens wide

When we shower it with kindness

As our love shines from inside.

Among the great and glorious gifts

  our heavenly Father sends

Is the gift of understanding

  that we find in loving friends,

For it's not money or gifts

  or material things,

But understanding the joy it brings,

That can change this old world

  in wonderful ways

And put goodness and mercy

  back in our days.

*Accept one another, then, just as Christ
accepted you, in order to bring praise to God.*

ROMANS 15:7

In this troubled world

it's refreshing to find

Someone who still has

the time to be kind,

Someone who still has

the faith to believe

That the more you give,

the more you receive,

Someone who's ready by

thought, word, or deed

To reach out a hand

in the hour of need.

THE UNEXPECTED KINDNESS FROM

AN UNEXPECTED PLACE,

A HAND OUTSTRETCHED IN FRIENDSHIP,

A SMILE ON SOMEONE'S FACE,

A WORD OF UNDERSTANDING

SPOKEN IN AN HOUR OF TRIAL

ARE UNEXPECTED MIRACLES THAT

MAKE LIFE MORE WORTHWHILE.

We do not know how it happened

in an hour of need

Somebody out of nowhere

proved to be a friend indeed.

For God has many messengers

we fail to recognize,

But He sends them when we need them

for His ways are wondrous wise!

It's not the things that can be bought

that are life's richest treasure,

It's just the little heart gifts

that money cannot measure. . .

A cheerful smile, a friendly word,

a sympathetic nod

Are priceless little treasures from

the storehouse of God.

Each time you smile,

    you'll find that it's true,

Somebody, somewhere

    will smile back at you.

And nothing on earth

    can make life more worthwhile

Than the sunshine and warmth

    of a beautiful smile.

Somehow in the generous heart

of loving, faithful friends

The good God in His charity

and wisdom always sends

A sense of understanding

and the power of perception

And mixes these fine qualities

with kindness and affection.

Friends and prayers are priceless treasures

Beyond all monetary measures,

And so I say a special prayer

That God will keep you in His care.

*"For where your treasure is,
there your heart will be also."*

MATTHEW 6:21

There is no garden so complete

But roses could make the place more sweet.

There is no life so rich and rare

But one more friend could enter there.

Like roses in a garden, kindness fills the air

With a certain bit of sweetness

as it touches everywhere.

Nothing on earth can make

life more worthwhile

Than a true, loyal friend and

the warmth of a smile,

For, just like a sunbeam makes

the cloudy days brighter,

The smile of a friend makes

a heavy heart lighter.

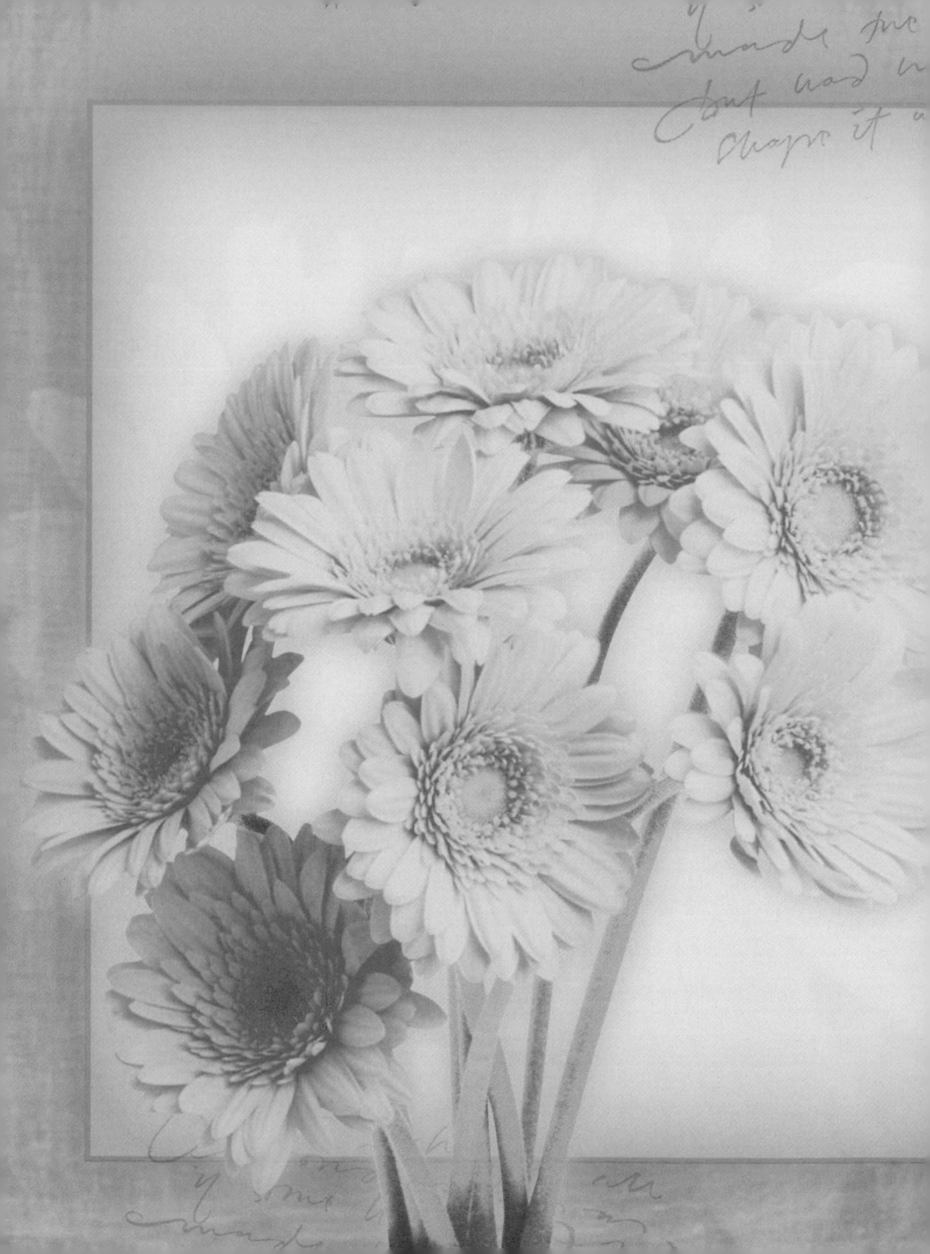

In Daily Living

*"I will see you again and
you will rejoice, and no one
will take away your joy."*

JOHN 16:22

God's blessings are all around us,
adorning our everyday lives. His constant
love and care. His promise to always be
with us. The wonders of His creation.
We might expect God to bless us when
our lives are through—if we have indeed
lived virtuous lives. But God blesses us in
the here and now, in the course of our
daily living. Receive His joy, for your God
has made you His own both in this life
and the never-ending life to come.

Since fear and dread and worry

cannot help in any way,

It's much healthier and happier

to be cheerful every day...

And if you'll only try it, you will find,

without a doubt,

A cheerful attitude's something

no one should be without.

Happiness is something we

   create in our minds—

It's not something you search for

   and so seldom find.

It's just waking up and beginning the day

By counting our blessings

   and kneeling to pray.

In the beauty of a snowflake,

Falling softly on the land,

Is the mystery and the miracle

Of God's great, creative hand.

God lives in the beauty

that comes with spring—

The colorful flower,

the birds that sing.

> *Give thanks to the LORD, for he is good.*
> *His love endures forever.*
>
> PSALM 136:1

When the heart is cheerful,

it cannot be filled with fear,

And without fear, the way ahead

seems more distinct and clear,

And we realize there's nothing

that we must face alone,

For our heavenly Father loves us,

and our problems are His own.

Thank You, God, for little things

that often come our way—

The things we take for granted

but don't mention when we pray—

The unexpected courtesy,

the thoughtful, kindly deed—

A hand reached out to help us

in the time of sudden need.

A little laughter, a little song,

A little teardrop

When things go wrong,

A little calm

And a little strife,

A little loving—

And that is life.

Yesterday's dead, tomorrow's unborn,
So there's nothing to fear
 and nothing to mourn,
For it's only the memory
 of things that have been
And expecting tomorrow
 to bring trouble again
That fills my today,
 which God wants to bless,
With uncertain fears
 and borrowed distress.
For all I need live for is
 this one little minute,
For life's here and now,
 and eternity's in it.

God gives us a power
    we so seldom employ,
For we're so unaware
    it is filled with such joy.
The gift that God gives us
    is anticipation,
Which we can fulfill
    with sincere expectation,
For there's power in belief
    when we think we will find
Joy for the heart
    and peace for the mind.
And believing the day
    will bring a surprise
Is not only pleasant
    but surprisingly wise.

If we open the door

to let joy walk through,

When we learn to expect

the best and most, too,

And believing we'll find

a happy surprise

Makes reality out of

a fancied surmise.

Into our lives come many things

   to break the dull routine—

The things we had not planned on

   that happen unforeseen—

The unexpected little joys

   that are scattered on our way,

Success we did not count on

   or a rare, fulfilling day.

Let us give ourselves away,

Not just today but every day,

And remember, a kind and thoughtful deed

Or a hand outstretched in a time of need

Is the rarest of gifts, for it is a part

Not of the purse but a loving heart;

And he who gives of himself will find

True joy of heart and peace of mind.

Sometimes when faith is running low

And I cannot fathom why things are so. . .

I walk among the flowers I grow

And learn the answers

to all I would know. . .

For among my flowers I have come to see

Life's miracle and its mystery,

And standing in silence and reverie,

My faith comes flooding back to me.

*Perfume and incense bring joy to the heart,
and the pleasantness of one's friend springs
from his earnest counsel.*

PROVERBS 27:9

Thank You for the miracles

    we are much too blind to see,

And give us new awareness

    of our many gifts from Thee,

And help us to remember that

    the key to life and living

Is to make each prayer a prayer of thanks

    and every day Thanksgiving.

Do not be anxious about anything, but in everything, by prayer and petition, with thanksgiving, present your requests to God.

PHILIPPIANS 4:6

America's beloved inspirational poet laurate, **Helen Steiner Rice,** has encouraged millions of people through her beautiful and uplifting verse. Born in Lorain, Ohio, in 1900, Helen was the daughter of a railroad man and an accomplished seamstress and began writing poetry at a young age.

In 1918, Helen began working for a public utilities company and eventually became one of the first female advertising managers and public speakers in the country. In January 1929, she married a wealthy banker named Franklin Rice, who later sank into depression during the Great Depression and eventually committed suicide. Helen later said that her suffering made her sensitive to the pain of others. Her sadness helped her to write some of her most uplifting verses.

Her work for a Cincinnati, Ohio, greeting card company eventually led to her nationwide popularity as a poet when her Christmas card poem "The Priceless Gift of Christmas," was first read on the Lawrence Welk Show. Soon Helen had produced several books of her poetry that were a source of inspiration to millions of readers.

Helen died in 1981, leaving a foundation in her name to offer assistance to the needy and the elderly. Now more than twenty-five years after her death, Helen's words still speak powerfully to the hearts of readers about love and comfort, faith and hope, peace and joy.